Weather on a Trip

by Louise Crary

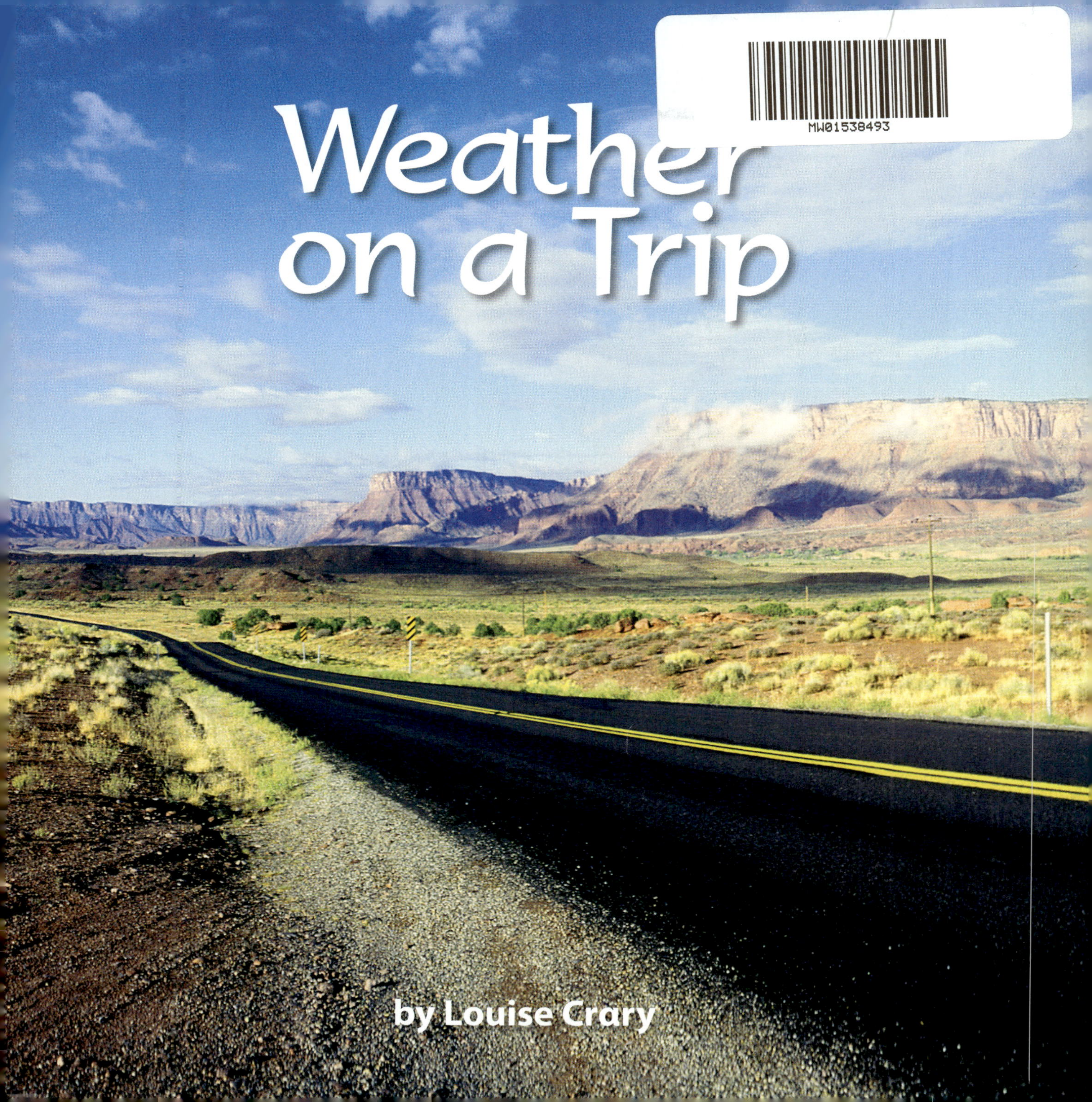

Waterford
Knox Lake
Ankenytown
Mohican Memorial State Forest
Nashville
Fredericktown
KNOX
Jelloway
Greer
Glenmont
Millersburg
Mt. Vernon
Mt. Vernon Nazarene College
Amity
Apple Valley Lake
Mount Vernon Developmental Center
Brinkhaven
Killbuck
Bangs
Kenyon College
Danville
Tiverton Center
Cavallo Station
Brandon
Blissfield
COSHOCTON
Walhonding
Walhonding
Utica
Warsaw
River
Louisville
Bedford
Tunnel Hill
Roscoe Village
Cooperdale
Vanatta
Rocky Fork
Wakatomika
Newark
Marne
Hanover
Baughman Park
Frazeysburg
Conesville
Adams Mills
Licking
Black Run
Heath
Black Hand Gorge
Dresden
Shannon
Nashport
MUSKINGUM
Muskingum
Flint Ridge
Dillon
Dillon Lake
Linnville
Brownsville
Gratiot
Hopewell
State Forest Nursery
Gilbert
Adamsville
O.U. Zanesville
Mt. Sterling
M.A.T.C.
Zanesville
Yost
Glenford
Zanesville Art Institute
Mt. Perry
"Y" Bridge
S. Zanesville
Norwich
Fultonham
Moxahala Park
Sego
National Rd. Zane Grey Museum
East Fultonham
Saltillo
Chandlersville
Redfield
Duncan Falls
Philo
Roseville
Cannelville
Blue Rock State Forest
Perry State Forest
Ohio Ceramic Center
Crooksville
Freeland
Merriam

The weather is sunny.

The weather is cloudy.

The weather is rainy.

The weather is stormy.

The weather is wonderful!